Cleo's Poem

By Sally Cowan

Cleo and Dad listened to a show as they were driving home.

Dad turned up the volume dial.

Young poets, send in your best poem for Poets Week!
You could win the chance to recite your poem on stage at the Town Hall!

Cleo was a poet!
She loved to read and
write poems.

But when she tried to write a
poem for the contest, her mind
went blank!
She could not think of a
winning topic.

Cleo sat on the couch with her sister, Zoe, who was watching a wildlife show.

A thought came to Cleo like a flashing neon light!

Cleo sat down to write her poem, and then Dad emailed it for her.

A week later, Dad got a reply.

But Cleo forgot she would have to read her poem to a crowd!

"A trial run will help with your nerves!" said Dad.

Cleo practised reading her poem to Dad, and she felt a lot better.

At the Town Hall, Cleo got up on stage.

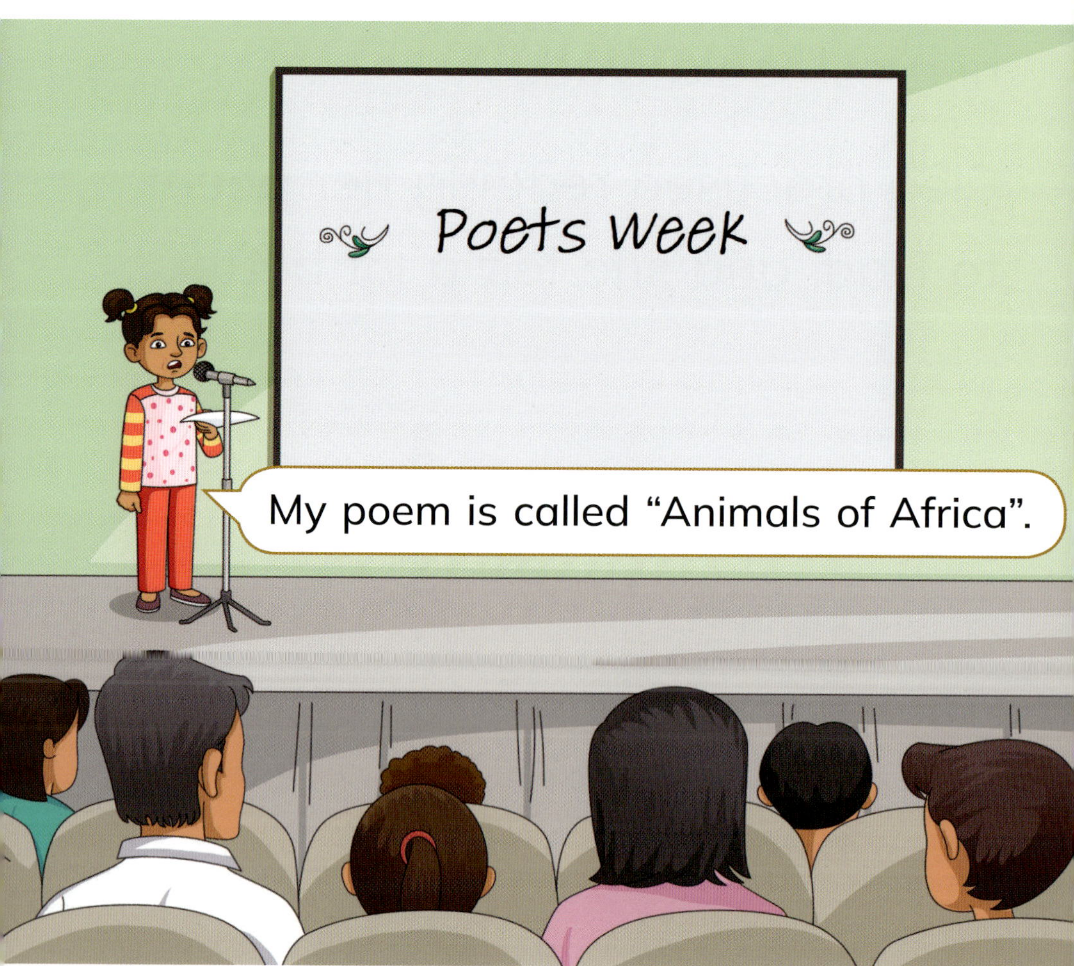

Animals of Africa

On the plains of Africa,
the lions flex their paws!

The lions' diet is all meat.
Check out their big, sharp
claws!

A zebra duo reacts with speed,
or they'll end up as dinner!
An elephant's too big to eat,
perhaps it is the winner!

They suck up fluid in their trunks
and spray it in a haze.

These giants of the great green plains
– indeed, they do amaze!

The crowd reacted by standing up and clapping.

Cleo's poem was a triumph!

CHECKING FOR MEANING

1. How did Cleo hear about the poetry contest? *(Literal)*
2. What happened at first when Cleo tried to write a poem for the contest? *(Literal)*
3. Where did Cleo get the idea for her poem? *(Inferential)*
4. How is a poem like a song? How is it different? *(Evaluative)*

EXTENDING VOCABULARY

trial	What did Dad mean by a *trial run*? What is another way the author could have said this?
flex	What does it mean to flex a paw? Can you flex your hand?
triumph	Does the word *triumph* mean something was a success or a failure? What is another way to say the same thing?

MOVING BEYOND THE TEXT

1. In the beginning, Cleo experienced something called "writer's block", which means she could not think of a good idea for her writing. Have you experienced writer's block (or another type of block that prevented you from starting or completing a project)? How did you get over it?

2. Have you ever felt nervous about doing something? What happened? How did you try to overcome your nerves?

3. Before Cleo went to the Town Hall, she practised reading her poem in front of Dad. Give an example of when people might need to practise for something.

4. Cleo asked Dad for help. Who have you asked for help when you were having trouble with something?

TIME TO WRITE

Write a short poem. Be sure to use rhyming words. You could write about animals like Cleo did or choose a different topic.